Gloria, Baby Ali, and Me

A TRUE STORY

UUKA ATO

Copyright © 2020 Uuka Ato
All rights reserved
First Edition

PAGE PUBLISHING, INC.
Conneaut Lake, PA

First originally published by Page Publishing 2020

ISBN 978-1-64628-754-3 (pbk)
ISBN 978-1-64628-755-0 (digital)

Printed in the United States of America

I met Gloria Jeanette Washington, my first true love of this highly educated African American woman. This very beautiful who lived with me for a very short time. The fall of 1971–spring 1972.

After I returned from my travels to Africa in August of 1971, I worked as part-time in the audiovisual department at Malcolm X Community College. It was during the registration period in the fall of 1971.

Gloria approached. "I'm here to take my student ID picture, can you help me?" she said.

I looked at her; she had a very beautiful smile on her face and a look in her eyes that I had only seen once in my life. That was the look and smile on Leah Nkulie's face—to whom I talk about in my book titled *My Story*.

In any event, I said yes. Give me your application and have a seat in this chair. She smiled and said okay with a bright look in her eyes. I took her picture twice.

She said, "Why did you take two pictures of me?"

"You're so lovely and beautiful. I will keep one for myself, if you don't mind. You can take another one for yourself if you want."

"That won't be necessary if you give me your telephone number and address. I will give you my telephone number, and you can call me later, and we will talk about me giving you my address."

I said, "Okay, that's good. I will call you in a few days or so."

She said, "Okay, but don't call me too late because I don't live alone. I live with my father and stepmother, and my stepmother don't like me very much."

"Will do," I said.

"There are other students waiting in line to have their pictures taken," she said.

I said, "Okay, I forgot."

The other students started laughing; we all laughed. Gloria and I said later we will talk more later this week.

"Okay, okay," she said, "remember don't call too late."

After a few days passed, I didn't see Gloria around the school or anywhere, I didn't want to call her too soon or anything. I couldn't stop thinking about her. I was afraid to call her because I didn't want her to think that I was too easy to get.

About a week later, I build up enough nerves to call. The voice on the other end said hello.

"I would like to speak to Gloria, please," I said.

"This is her speaking," the voice on the other end said. "Who are you?"

"This is Hassoun, the brother from Malcolm X College, who took your picture."

"I know," she said.

"What took you so long to call me?" she said.

"I've been very busy with my work and studies."

"I understand," she said.

"I have a full-time job and part-time schedule, I couldn't go to school because I have to work as much as I can."

"What kind of work do you do?" I said.

"I'm an executive secretary at Steward-Warner," she said, "I'm trying to make as much as I can so I can move out, get my own apartment or place to stay."

I told Gloria that I had my own apartment, and once we get to know each other, we could share an apartment, we could be roommates.

Gloria said, "That's a good idea, I must get out of my father's and stepmother's house."

We talked about half an hour or so. Gloria said that she had to be at work early tomorrow, and she had a couple of classes tomorrow evening. After classes, she would come to the audiovisual department and talk about us becoming roommates.

I said, "Okay, that sounds great."

The next day after her classes, she came to the AV department. She stayed until I got off work. When we were leaving, I asked Gloria where did she live.

She said, "I line on the west side or out west. I take the B train on L from Damen St., southwest to Cermak St. (Twenty-Second Street) where I get off at Homan St and takes the Homan St. bus north to Westend St. where I get off and walk about one block to my father's and stepmother's house."

I told her that I lived on Parkside St. and Washington Boulevard.

I took the A train L to Central Avenue (5600 W) where I get off and took the Central Avenue bus to Washington Boulevard, got off and walked about one block west to Parkside St., where I stayed. I told Gloria that she would get home faster if she took the A train L instead of taking the B train L because the A train L travels straight west and the B train L travels southwest, taking her further south. I don't know too much about these trains travels. I told her that we could take the train (L) together, and she could see for herself.

"Okay," she said.

We got on the A train (L) and to her great surprise, she saw how much time she saved by taking the A train. After we arrived to her father's and stepmother's house, I walked her to the door, she said, "Don't talk too loud you may wake someone up. They will be too nosy."

I said, "Okay, I'm not going to stay long."

After we got to the door, I took her into my arms and kissed her softly on the lips. She smiled and kissed me back, and we quietly said that we will see each other in a few days.

"You know I only have classes three days a week. I will call you from work to see if I can come by your apartment to look around to see if it is big enough for us or two people to live in."

I said, "Okay."

She went into the house, I turned around and saw a bus coming. I ran to the bus stop on Washington Boulevard, west. For the next few days, I didn't or talk to Gloria, but I continued to think about her. I had a lot on my mind with graduation, finals, other females who wanted to stay with me but couldn't help financially or help pay for anything, they just wanted to move or get out of their parents' house. I was having a hard time paying bills. I was hoping to find a female roommate who would or could come live with me as a roommate only. However, in the case of Gloria, I liked her, and she had a great job, and she was beautiful and more than willing to pay her way and help me in other ways (such as cooking and helping with my studies). She was precisely what I wanted, not only wanted but what I needed. However, Gloria had her own method for accomplishing something or intends of which I didn't share or interested. I learned later that every female I dated, they all had on things in mind, or should I say two (children and marriage), and not necessary in that order.

Please don't misunderstand me. I was deeply in love with Gloria, but I didn't want to have children, marry her or anyone else at this time. In any event, about two weeks later, Gloria and I became roommates only at first. Things was going very well. We shared a lot of things together. When other friends would call the house for me, Gloria would tell me about these calls. She would tell me that she didn't care that they (females) call or not; however, she said that she wished they would not call me every day and not call so late at night because she works every day, and the calls at night woke her up. She was right, of course. I told Gloria that I would tell my friends, males and females, to stop calling me late at night and not to call me every day. For a few weeks, things were okay there were very few calls. After the calls started coming in again, Gloria told me I should change my telephone number. I didn't want to change my number, so Gloria and I got into arguments. I told Gloria that we were only roommates so what was it to her if other females did call me.

Gloria said, "That's not true, you know we are and have been much more than roommates, and you know that's to be the fact. I do everything for you [such as cooking, paying bills, washing clothes, and yes, sex]. I do all these things for you, and you disrespect me. My grandmother who lives in Missouri, I told her about you and your female friends. She told me to tell you to forget about those old friends. She told me that you and me ought to get married before I end up pregnant or something."

Gloria's grandmother, on her mother's side, lived in Kansas City, Missouri, where I believed that Gloria was born—September, 5, 1950. She had one brother who's older than her, I think. In any event, Gloria's grandmother and mother were some very evil and wicked people, they were always causing trouble between us. They didn't like Gloria stayed with her father and stepmother in Chicago since she was six years old or so. As stated before, Gloria's stepmother, grandmother, and mother didn't like her. In fact, her mother gave her up to her father to live with when she was very young. That's how she ended up staying in Chicago, Illinois.

In any event, as time passed, Gloria and I started to get along very well. I changed my telephone number. The friends (females) stopped coming by, with the exception of one or two friends. Things began to improve between us, but on some occasions, Gloria talked about having children, three or more, and getting married someday. I would tell her the same thing, but I really didn't want to get married or have any kids. She would get very angry with me. I recall once that her mother and grandmother called and told me why I didn't want to get married or have children by anyone yet. Maybe someday Gloria and I will get married after I finish my schooling. Her grandmother got very angry with me. She said I should let her go so she could find somebody that would marry her. I told them that if Gloria wanted to leave me and find someone to marry, she was free to go. They became very angry with me. Her grandmother, who I believe I was talking to, hung up the phone.

When Gloria came home from work, I would tell her about her grandmother calling, trying to force me to marry her. Gloria would get angry. I recall her telling me when her mother or grandmother called me, if I answered the phone, just to listen and not to say anything, they are trying to break us up. I just said okay.

As time passed, Gloria and I would go out to the movies, dinner, etc. Sometimes, we would visit my mother, Eleanor Anderson, and my sister, Veola Tucker, who lived on the Southside at 8512 South Ada, with her husband, Thomas Tucker. Also residing there were their children, Thomas Tucker Jr. (whom we call Bird), Lynette Tucker, Lawanda Tucker, Bruce Tucker, and Cyrus Tucker. They all were some nice and respectful children. I recall one day, Gloria and I went to the movie (I can't recall the movie we saw), this time, we took my youngest brother with us (Carillo Anderson). Gloria and I got into an argument about something of which I can't recall what. It may have been something related to us getting married or she was upset because my brother was with us or she may have been pregnant at the time.

In any event, she said something that I didn't like. What she said I didn't take it kindly, so I slapped her in the face a couple of times of which I greatly regret. She started crying and said that she wanted to go home. I said, "Okay, fine." My brother, Carrillo, just looked at me in shock. After we left the movie theater, on the bus (or as we called it), we made certain that Carillo got home, then we called a cab and went home. After we got home, I told Gloria that I was sorry that I hit her. She said that it was okay. Later on that night, we made great love to each other. Everything was forgotten, or so we thought.

A few days later, Gloria's grandmother called. Gloria answered the phone.

"Hello, Grandmom, fine, we are okay."

At this point, Gloria turned to me.

"This is for you. It's my grandmother. She wants to talk to you."

Before she gave the phone, Gloria said, "Please, Soun," that is what she called me instead of calling me Hassoun, "don't say anything. Just listen, please." She repeated, "Please."

I said, "Okay, give me the phone."

I took the phone.

"Hello," I said.

"Hello," her grandmother said. "When are you Gloria going to get married? Do you know she's pregnant?"

"No, I don't."

"What you're trying to say it's not yours?"

I said, "No. Gloria didn't tell me that she is pregnant."

"She must have a good reason if she didn't tell you. Let me talk back to Gloria."

I said, "Yes, Grandmom," and hung up the phone.

I asked Gloria what's wrong.

She said, "I think I missed my period or monthly cycle."

"You should have told me. It's okay, we will work out something."

She smiled and said, "Okay. Are you not angry with me because I told my mother and grandmother and not you?"

"No, I'm not. Everything will work out for the best."

Gloria became very happy. She went into the kitchen and started to cook dinner. The next day, she got up very early and cooked breakfast. She couldn't cook very well, but that was okay. She had many other qualities. I left for school about one hour after her. We both took the CTA because we didn't own an automobile or anything. We were two young people in love.

As time passed, Gloria started to have stomach pains. The pain started when she was in her fourth month of pregnancy. After she return home from work, she would get about one hour of rest then she would get up and try to make or fix dinner, but she couldn't because of the pain. I told her it was okay don't push yourself too much. I will fix or cook dinner and all the other meals for us. She smiled and said thank you. However, on occasions, Gloria would get up and fix meals in spite of the pains in her stomach. I recall one morning, she attempted to fix breakfast. I repeated to her not to hurt herself or the baby. Gloria however continued to do things around the house.

One day, I told her to stop pushing herself too much, and she responded by saying, "This is your apartment, and I'm living here, so I have to help you keep the apartment clean."

That was how Gloria was. She was dedicated and wanted to help me too much that she did everything and more for me. Why she even dropped out of school and took another job to help us live better (I had a part-time job at Malcolm X College that was nowhere near enough). She told me to stay in school and get my degree.

After I finished school, she would go back and get her degree. Gloria's first job was at Advance Process Supply. She made $105 per week from 1971 to 1972, Stewart Warner made $127 per week from April to December 1972. Finally, Gloria's pain was so intense that she had to stop working and apply for unemployment benefits. Her pains were excruciating. I took her to the emergency doctor (she didn't have a family doctor). We just went to any doctor. The doctors we saw wouldn't give her anything for the pains because they said the pain medicine may harm or hurt the baby. Eventually, we did get a doctor to prescribe some pain medicines for her, but the pain medicines didn't do any good (or very little). We went to different doctors. None of them would prescribe or give her any stronger pain medicines. I recall going to some doctor out west in Maywood, Illinois.

The doctor of whom I don't remember his name, in any event, the doctor gave her a stronger prescription for her pain.

He said, "You can take this to any Walgreen's Pharmacy and get this."

We took the prescription and left. At this time, we're living on 8156 S. Hermitage St. on the 1st floor. So we went to the Walgreen's on Seventy-Ninth Street and Ashland Avenue. After waiting about one and a half hours, the prescription was ready. We walked up to the desk.

"I'm Gloria. Are my prescriptions ready?"

The pharmacist said, "Let me see your ID."

Gloria showed the pharmacist her work ID, paid for it, and we left. Gloria was very tired and angry. She started crying and said, "I don't think that I should take this medicine because it may hurt or harm the baby."

I said, "It's up to you."

Gloria said that it was my fault that she was pregnant.

"I should have listened to my mother and grandmother; you don't care about me. If you did," she continued, "you will marry me."

As we walked, she started walking very slow.

I said, "Hurry up, let's make this light."

The light was green. She continued to walk at a slow pace. I reached and took her by the hand.

"Come on, come on," I repeated.

The light was about to change. A car was coming fast. I reached and took Gloria by the arm. In the process, she dropped the bottle in the streets and the oncoming car ran over the medicine breaking the bottle open. The pills was all over the streets.

"What are you going to do now?" I asked. "We don't have any money left to pay for any more medication."

Gloria said, "It's okay. I really don't want to take those pills anyway because they may cause harm or hurt our baby. In a few months or so I will the baby. The pains I will take."

I said, "Okay, I understand."

As time passed, Gloria was having pains in her stomach. However, she was able to bear it. Once a week or so, the pain would make her stay away from work. The rest of the week, she would be fine. Her mother and grandmother continued to asked and begged me to let Gloria come down to Kansas City, Missouri, until she have the baby.

"We want to see our grandbaby. Please, please, send her here. After the baby is born, she can return back to Chicago alone with the baby."

Things will be okay. I would tell Gloria everything they said. Gloria would say no sound.

"Please, don't send me down there. You don't know how they are. They are some mean, wilky people. They don't care anything about you or me. They're trying to break us up. They only want their grandchild."

As the days and weeks passed, Gloria continued to do the best she could with her pregnancy and walking a narrow line with her mother and grandmother. I recall one day sitting around, talking about her going to Kansas City, Missouri, to have our baby.

"You can stay with them for a short time or at least until our baby is born. Afterward, you can move back here (Chicago) the baby, you and me will live together. We can grow old together (a statement that Gloria will say to me on many occasions; we can have two or three more children).

I responded by saying "Yes, maybe after I finish college with a bachelor or master's degree. We can get married and everything can work out fine. I agreed; however, in the meantime, what are we going to do about your mother and grandmother? I would like to make them happy. I will call them and tell them that you can come to Kansas City and have the baby. Afterward, in a few weeks or so, you and the baby will return back to Chicago to me."

Gloria said, "I don't think that it would be that easy, you don't know how they are. They are some coldhearted people, low-down dirty folks."

I said, "Okay. If we stick together, nothing or no one can keep us apart. I don't want to live with them no matter what you say. I know how low down they are."

Gloria began to cry. "I don't want to leave you here. Who will take care of you?" she said, "cook, help pay the rent, wash your clothing, etc.?"

"I can do all those things myself. It only be for a short time, three weeks or so. It will be okay as long as we stick to our plan."

The next week went by slowly. Gloria was getting her things together to go to Kansas City. She continued to tell me not to send her to Kansas City.

"I don't want to go. Please, please, don't make me go, I don't want to leave you."

"I promised your mother that you would be there in a week or so. Your mother been nice to me. She begged me to send you there so you can have her first grandchild with her or them (her grandmother and her). I gave your mother my word, and I never break it."

In any event, a week later, I took Gloria to the trailway bus station (downtown Chicago) on East Randolph Street. We called a taxicab. However, no one showed up, so we took the Madison Street bus. After we got on the bus with three or four suitcases (luggage), Gloria started crying.

"Please, please, don't make me go. I don't want to go. Please, Soun [Hassoun for short]."

At this point, Gloria was over eight months pregnant.

"I will see you in about a month or so. I will be coming to Kansas City to pick you and our baby up. We will be together as we both planned."

I didn't know at that time that her mother and grandmother had plans to never let Gloria, the baby, and me get together again.

In any event, in all these years (forty-five), I can see Gloria on the trailway bus. As the bus pulled away from the station, Gloria started crying and pleading to me don't make her go. This was one of the greatest mistakes I ever made in my life. Gloria told me not to send her away, but I didn't listen. When Gloria arrived to Kansas City about ten hours later, she called me.

"I'm here safe. I'm tired now, so I will call you after I have rested."

I said, "Okay."

We hung up. Before Gloria gave birth to our baby (son), we talked to each other almost every day. She would tell me how much she misses me, and she will be very happy when we are together again with one addition—the baby, me, and her. I told her I will be very happy also. The baby was born about three weeks later. After baby Ali was born, there was some serious setback with his health. He had a serious heart condition. The doctor had to install in his chest a pacemaker to keep him alive at the tender age of nine days.

Our son (Baby Ali) was born on February 6, 1973. We were very happy, but as I stated above, our son was born with a serious heart condition. He would have to stay in the hospital, so more tests could be done or ran. I became very worried. I asked her was she okay, and she said she was fine but felt depressed because of the condition of our son, Baby Ali.

"The baby would be all right. Everything will be…to save Baby Ali life…will be done," she said softly.

I said, "Okay. I'm going to hang up now so you can get some rest but before we hang up, why didn't your mother or grandmother call and tell me that you had given birth?"

She said very emotionally, "I thought that they would, but they some evil people and don't like you very much. I had overheard them saying bad things about you. They told me that if I go back to Chicago with you, that I would be a big fool."

I didn't know it at the time, but shortly I realized that all this (me sending her [Gloria] to Kansas City so the baby can be born down here with them was a plan to break us up). Her mother and grandmother would do anything to keep our son among them even if it meant that Gloria and I would break up. I didn't see this until he was over three months old. Two weeks after Baby Ali was born, I the Greyhound bus line. I went down to Kansas City, Missouri, to pick up Gloria and Baby Ali to bring them back to Chicago, Illinois. In addition, I wanted to meet her mother and grandmother because all the time, Gloria was living with them several times, and they appear to be friendly. We never talked long, but we talked about Gloria and I getting married and possibly living in Kansas City. If we did get married, we certainly would not live in Kansas City.

After talking to them, I would talk with Gloria and mention the things that her mother and grandmother would say to me. She said the marriage is okay, but living in Kansas City was not her plans. As mentioned above, Gloria's plan as the one that we agreed to, which was after the birth of our son, I'm coming to get her and our son and return back to Chicago. I can't to you about our plans because she was in her mother's house and family members are listening to our conversation. I said okay. We hung up.

On occasion however, she would go out on a pay phone and call me collect. I told her I was coming down to pick them up the coming weekend and to meet her mother, afterward she could say goodbye, and we would return to Chicago. She said okay. We said "goodbye" and "I love you." The coming week, I went down to Kansas City to pick Gloria and Baby Ali up. I couldn't wait to get there, but when I got there, to my astonishment, Gloria's mother told her to tell me that I was not welcome to her house. The exact words Gloria said was that her mother said "If that nigga step foot in my house, I will blow his head off."

I didn't know what for the past few weeks was very nice and respectful toward me by telephone. Now all of a sudden, she wants my blood. In any event, I didn't go to her house. Gloria met me at the bus station and bought Baby Ali with her. She also gave me an article from the *Kansas City Times* that shocked me to the core of my being. The article was about Baby AM and written by Rosalind K. Ellingsworth, science pediatric heart specialist at Children's Mercy Hospital. The article stated the following CMH successfully implanted an electronic pacemaker in a nine-day-old baby whose heart was unable to beat normally. The infant was admitted to the hospital when he was a day old suffering from congestive heart failure—the inability of the heart to effectively contract and pump blood. The infant's heart was only beating thirty times a minute. To get the heart to beat more regularly and effectively, a tiny battery powered device was surgically placed in the body. Dr. Thomas M. Holder, the pediatric surgeon, who operated on the baby, explained it is extremely rare for a newborn to develop congestive heart failure and that is just as rare for a pacemaker to be implanted in a day old child.

"We certainly are not the first to perform this procedure," Dr. Holder said, "but it is unusual for a child to be suffering from this condition at this early age. Usually, children don't get congestive heart failure before they are a year old."

Dr. Holder said that at first, heart-stimulating drugs were used to get the child's heart to beat normally and when he was admitted to Children's Mercy, an external pacemaker was placed on his chest to send electric stimulation to the heart. Both methods failed. Dr. Holder explained that the external pacemaker is not preferred for long-term stimulation of the heart muscles because the charge it delivers stimulates other body muscles as well as the heart. Heart specialists at the hospital knew that the condition is usually a result of some anatomical defect in the heart, which occurred because of improper development during gestation; however, tests ran on the infant showed no anatomical defect. Dr. Holder said that the angiograms performed showed an anatomically heart because there appeared to be no defect in the structure of the infant's heart; the physician assumed his condition was due to some congenital defect in the nerves, which triggered the heart muscles.

However, Dr. Holder, there was no way to verify the assumption without actually cutting into the heart nerves and taking a part of the neural tissue for laboratory analysis. The second day that Baby AM was in the hospital, the physicians put in place a transvenous pacemaker, which caused Baby AM less discomfort. This device performed the same duties of regularly stimulating the heart electrically but was only a temporary solution. Dr. Holder said the physicians waited a week to see if Baby AM's heart might begin beating regularly on its own.

"Occasionally, the heart of these children will convert on their own," Dr. Holder noted, "but in this case, (baby) didn't happen."

The doctors decided on surgery. The pacemaker implanted in Baby Ali was smaller than those used in adults and contained only two batteries instead of four in the adult models. Dr. Holder explained that the surgery required no special techniques and was no open heart surgery. The chest walls were open to exposed the heart and a thin wire was passed into one of the heart's chambers. The battery pack was placed under the skin of the abdomen to send electric pulses through the wire to the heart muscle. The pacemaker implanted in Baby Ali was further modified to allow for fast-paced growth of Baby Ali during the first months of life. Dr. Holder said the wire-carrying electric impulse would "play out" as Baby Ali grows. The one difficulty with pacemakers in 1973 medical science at that time had not been able to develop batteries that lasted longer than two years. Dr. Holder said that Baby Ali would be brought to the hospital for regular checkup and would have to undergo a change of battery about every two years. This would only however involve opening the skin over the battery pack.

The wire carrying the electric pulse to the heart eventually would have to be replaced or have an extension put on it as he grows. Dr. Holder said Baby Ali had experienced no difficulties since the surgery and was ready to go home. After reading this medical report, I was very sad. It hurt me greatly to learn that my son was born with congested heart failure and in order to stay alive, he needed a pacemaker. However, I was (am) very happy that my son would be able to live with the advancements in medical science. My son would be able to live if all the rules are followed, but I have to make a great decision as far as taking Gloria and Baby Ali back with me to Chicago, Illinois. This decision had to be made quickly. Gloria and I discussed the situation. We were at a crossroad or impasse. We couldn't decide what we should do. So with great reluctance, we decided to include her grandmother.

Her grandmother said quickly, "You should leave Gloria and the baby here in KC where his doctors are. So if there are any problems, the doctors know his history."

At this time, I didn't know anything about Children's Memorial Hospital in Chicago. So Gloria and I discussed the situation some more and decided that they should stay here for another month or two or until I look into the Children's Memorial Hospital in Chicago. I only stayed one day. I had to get back to Chicago and my studies. It was during midterms. Gloria and I agreed that I would return back and pick them up in another month or so. I kissed her and Baby Ali bye-bye. I see them later and left.

After returning to Chicago, I called Gloria almost every day to see how Baby Ali was doing. Everything was going fine.

"I will be down there to get you and Baby Ali in about a month."

She agreed and said that she couldn't wait to get away from her mother because there was a lot of problems living with her. Finally another month passed. I called and told Gloria that I was coming to get them on Saturday. She said when I got there, she wanted to talk to me about something that was very important. I said okay and hung up the telephone.

On Saturday, I purchased a bus ticket to Kansas City with the hope of bringing Gloria and Baby Ali back with me. When I got there, Gloria met me at the bus station. To my surprise, she told me that she had moved out of her mother's house and that she had found a job and had been working the past two weeks (something that she never told me during our conversation on the phone). She said that since I didn't have a job in Chicago, that we could live down there. I could find a job and finish my college education in KC. I know that I didn't want to live in KC, and I was certain that Gloria didn't want to live there either. I was greatly confused and shocked.

Had her mother, grandmother, or someone else gotten to her and convinced her that staying in KC with them would be better than staying in Chicago with me? Gloria said that she and Baby Ali wanted to return with me, but she needed more time to think about it. I told her that we have been apart for about two months, and it was for us to reunite.

"What about our plans?" I said. The plans were good but I didn't anticipate finding a job. Plus she said that we could get married and live in KC. I told her that I didn't want to live in KC. She said she didn't either but added that she had found a pretty good job and apartment that was small, but we could find one larger later on after I found a job. At this point, a male friend of her family came over and told us that he was ready to take us to his new apartment. Baby Ali was sitting in a baby seat in the back. He was asleep so I didn't wake him up. We got into the car, and the friend of the family drove off. He appeared to be upset about something.

Later on, I discovered who this friend really was. In any event, when we arrived to the new apartment, the movers were about to finished moving Gloria's furniture into the apartment. Gloria paid them and the left. The so-called friend of the family said that he would see me later and that he would come back and take me to see the rest of KC. I said okay. He turned and said something to Gloria and left. We went into the apartment with Baby Ali who was still asleep. Gloria and I started to move the furniture around. At this point, Gloria's grandmother appeared. Gloria had told me that her grandmother was coming by to meet me and that her grandmother was angry and hard to get along with. She said that her mother and grandmother were two of a kind. She said that if her grandmother talk smart to me not to get angry. Just say what she wants to hear. She told me that after a month or so that she would return to Chicago with me. The true reason why she moved was that she couldn't stay with her grandmother and mother any longer. The job, she liked it, but she could find another job in Chicago or even return to her old job at Baird & Warner.

I said, "Okay, I will not say anything to upset your grandmother. If she offends me, I will refrain myself."

At this point, her grandmother came up and knocked on the front door. Gloria opened the door. The grandmother walked in, and I was holding Baby Ali (he was wake now). I walked over to greet her grandmother.

I said, "Hello, I'm glad to meet you."

The grandmother looked at me with anger in her eyes and said, "What are you going to do? Keep running in and out until Gloria have another baby?"

She wouldn't shake my hand. I looked over at Gloria. Gloria shook her head as to say please don't say anything. The grandmother took Baby Ali out of my hands and said he's a very handsome baby and handed the baby to Gloria.

"How long are you going to stay?" she asked me.

Before I could reply, she said, "Never mind, don't answer. You both can do whatever you want to do," in a very offensive voice.

With that, she turned and left.

"What is her problem?"

Gloria said her grandmother and mother hated me, and they don't want me to take their great-grandson and grandson away from them. Gloria repeated her and Baby Ali would join me later in another month or so in Chicago and that I would have to come and pick them up. I said okay. I asked Gloria what happened to this friend who was supposed to return and take me around to see more of KC. Gloria said he is not coming back with a deep fear in her voice. She said that she had gone out with him a few times but told him that I was her man and when I come, he would have to go. It was nothing serious between them, and he understood that. I told her that she should not have gone out with him or anyone else. You knew that you and I were still together. She agreed and started crying. She said that she was sorry. I told her this is another reason why we must return to Chicago as soon as possible before something serious happen. Gloria agreed. She said after no longer than a month, we would reunite in Chicago. I agreed. She didn't have a babysitter, so she asked me will I stay with her for a few days or so as long as I could or until she found a babysitter.

Her grandmother and mother was out of the question. I told her that it was between semester break and I will stay for at least a week. She said okay, that's good. Gloria cooked dinner, and I played with our son in the living room. About 9:00 p.m., someone called Gloria on the telephone. Gloria answered. I heard a voice on the other end say, "Get that nigger out of your apartment, or I will get him out." I heard his voice very clearly. At first, I thought this was her mother or grandmother trying to frighten me. However, shortly after Gloria hung up, she told me who it was. It was this so-called friend of the family. It was Eddie. The guy, who she had gone out with or dated a few times.

Gloria said she had borrowed some money from him and that he was coming over to get it back and that he had a gun with him in the event that I get in the way. I only looked at Gloria and said these are some of the problems that people get into when they start sneaking around with other people. She repeated the above that he wanted the money back that he gave her.

"How much did he give you?" I asked.

"Forty dollars," she said.

I gave her the forty dollars.

"When he come, give it to him, and tell him not to return."

She called Eddie on the phone and told him to come pick up the money. About an hour later, he came up to the door and knocked. When Gloria answered who is it, "I have a gun," the voice said. "And I want my money."

Gloria was afraid to open the door. I said open the door Gloria and throw the money at him. Gloria quickly cracked the door open and quickly threw the money at him. Eddie took the money and left. The rest of the night, Gloria and I talked about getting away from KC as soon as possible. I asked Gloria if she knew where Eddie lived, and she said yes. I asked her to give me his address. She did.

As it turned out, he only lived four or five blocks from her. I was very angry at Eddie for endangering the lives of Baby Ali, Gloria, and me. I showed her a gun that I had brought with me.

She became very frightened and said, "What are you going to do with that?"

"Nothing, I just wanted you to know that you and Baby Ali were protected all along."

She asked, "That's why you weren't afraid for me to open the door?"

I said, "Right. I was hoping he walked in."

After a while, we went to bed. The next day was Sunday, and I got up early. Gloria and Baby Ali were sleeping. I went out to try to find Eddie's apartment. I first went the wrong way. I asked a fellow on the street where was this street I had written down on a sheet of paper (Eddie's address). The fellow said two blocks this way, he pointed to my right. I thanked him and walked in the direction he pointed in. Gloria had given me Eddie's street name, number, and apartment number. When I got there, I rang the bell once, and no one answered. I rang the bell again. Still no one answered. Eddie lived on the 1st floor, so I walked around the side and knocked on the window a couple of times. Still no one answered. I waited outside of Eddie's apartment for about five minutes with the hope that I see Eddie coming or leaving his apartment so I could do to him what he said he was going to do to me—shoot him (or take him out).

Eddie didn't show up. It was a good thing that he didn't because I was going to take him out for threatening my baby, my queen (woman), and me. In any event, I returned back to Gloria's apartment about half an hour later. Gloria was washing up in the bathroom. When she came out, she asked, "Where have you been?"

"For a short walk," I said.

"I thought that you had gone to find Eddie," she said.

I said, "No, I only went for a short walk," I repeated. The rest of the day passed quickly. The remainder of the week went slowly. Gloria went to work every day while I babysat our son. Baby Ali was about three months, and he cried a lot when Gloria left for work, but eventually he would stop crying and went to sleep after I fed him.

One day, while Gloria was at work, her mother came by with a couple of small children. I told her that Gloria hadn't come home from work yet (this was the first and only time that I saw her mother). She didn't stay long; however, she stayed two or three minutes. Gloria came in a half hour later, and I told her that her mother came by with a couple of small children. I told her that she said she came by to see Baby Ali and that she only stayed a few minutes.

When Gloria returned to the apartment from work, she would be very tired. Sometimes, she would be too tired to cook dinner. I told her that it was okay. That if she told me what she wanted to eat, I would cook (or fix) it for her. As what stated above, the days went by slowly. Finally, the last day was on a Saturday. I got up and packed my suitcase as we sat around and talked about when her and Baby Ali will be moving to Chicago. I became very sad. I did not want to leave Gloria and my (our) son in KC. Gloria didn't want me to leave. We agreed that this separation wouldn't be for no more than a month. Gloria called a taxi to take me to the bus station. Before the taxi arrived, we talked about the possibility of us living in KC. I didn't take it too seriously because KC was a small city, and I didn't know anyone down here. Plus Gloria didn't know anybody down here but her grandmother and mother who didn't care anything about her, but they did love and care Baby Ali, when her mother named him Kenneth (a name that I hated).

In any event, the taxi arrived. Gloria and Baby Ali rode with me to the station. After we got there, we got out of the taxi. I paid the driver. Gloria and the baby also got out. I took my luggage from the trunk of the taxi. We walked inside of the bus station and waited until the departure to Chicago was announced. I kissed my son and Gloria goodbye and told them we will be reunited again soon in Chicago. Gloria started crying, my eyes were watery too, but I couldn't cry in front of Gloria (however, after I got out of sight of Gloria, I did cry later). I told her that if we stayed with our plans, we would be together again in a short time. I got on the bus, waved to Gloria and my son. I didn't think in a zillion years that this would be the last time I would see Gloria and my son in person.

In the days and weeks to come, I would talk to Gloria almost every day. She would put Baby Ali on the phone to talk, but all he could say was dada, mama, etc. Two weeks later, I called and asked Gloria was she ready to come to Chicago. She (to my surprise) said why can't I move down to KC. I told her that I couldn't move down there. She asked if I have a job. I told her no. She said why can't I relocate. I told her that I was still going to college, and I had a part-time job in college. We would get into arguments about what was best for the baby and us. I told Gloria that she allowed her mother and grandmother to persuade her into staying in KC. I told her that maybe she started going out with Eddie again. She denied that emphatically. She started talking about the time I hit her and the times old girlfriends called the house. I told her that was all in the past. She didn't believe me.

These arguments would happen every time I called her. I told her that if we were going to reunite, it had to be in Chicago. She said why do it have to be in Chicago, we can live here in Kansas City, Missouri. This just went on and on and felt us drifting farther and farther apart. I sent money order to help buy things for baby AM. One day, my money order came back written on the side of the envelope was moved address unknown. I attempted to contact Gloria, but her phone number was changed. I attempted to call her mother, but her mother's number was also changed. I wanted to return to Kansas City to see if I could find them (Gloria and Baby Ali), but I never did because the money order and letter I wrote her was returned whereabout unknown. The more I looked at the writing on the envelope, it appeared to be Gloria's handwritings. I know Gloria's handwriting because I compared it to other handwritings of hers. I also showed the return letters to my sister, and my sister also concluded that the writings appeared to be Gloria's.

Me & Baby Ali

The birth of the Baby Ali

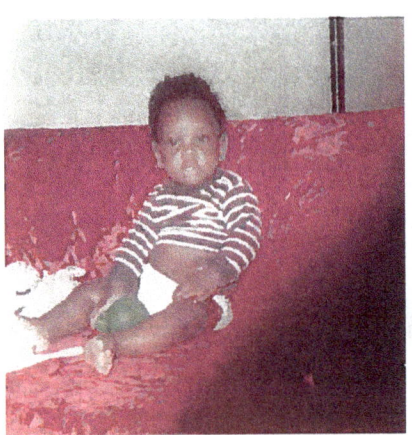
Baby Ali (2 mos)

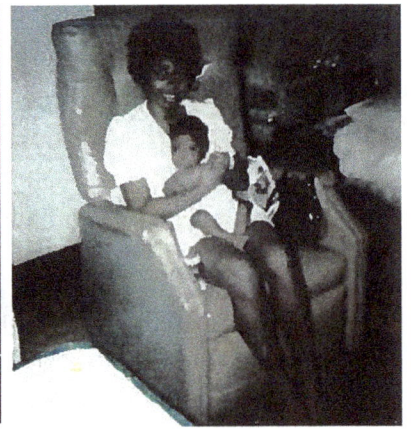
Gloria & Baby Ali (2 mos)
1971

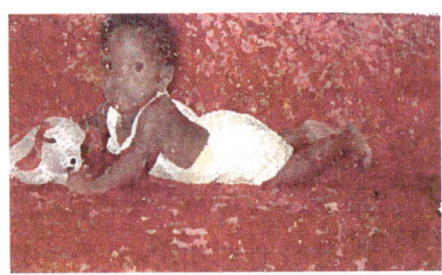

About the Author

A brief biographical sketch of Uuka Umi Ato, beginning with the most recent.

The author of My Story (2018).

Master of arts degree in Urban Studies; Concordia University, River Forest, II (1994).

Bachelor of arts of Psychology, Chicago State University (1976).

Diploma in arts, Malcolm X Junior College (1972).

Ged Diploma, University of Southern II (1969).

Skinned Elementary School no diploma. I was kicked out because of my age. On 1960, I think I was seventeen years of age.

First love, Gloria J. Washington, 1971–1972. One child, Baby Ali, who her mother named Kenneth. You can learn more about Baby Ali in my story (2018).

CPSIA information can be obtained
at www.ICGtesting.com
Printed in the USA
BVHW010920180220
572579BV00022BA/1985